Healthy Brain and Body Habits for Kids

Developing Healthy Habits to Make Your Kids
Physically and Mentally Strong

By

GoldInk Books

BEFORE YOU START READING, DOWNLOAD YOUR FREE DIGITAL ASSETS!

Be sure to visit the URL below on your computer or mobile device to access the free digital asset files that are included with your purchase of this book.

These digital assets will complement the material in the book and are referenced throughout the text.

DOWNLOAD YOURS HERE:

www.GoldInkBooks.com

Respective authors own all copyrights not held by the publisher.

The information herein is offered for informational purposes solely and is universal as so. The presentation of the information is without contract or any type of guarantee assurance.

The trademarks that are used are without any consent, and the publication of the trademark is without permission or backing by the trademark owner. All trademarks and brands within this book are for clarifying purposes only and are owned by the owners themselves, not affiliated with this document.

Table of Contents

Introduction

Do you know almost half of the time you are awake; you are on autopilot?

Researchers have found out that 45% of our daily activities are based on habits. Some studies by cognitive psychologists and neurobiologists even indicate that 40 to 95% of human behavior, i.e., how we think, what we say, and our overall actions fall into the category of habit. This might force you to think, "What kind of autopilot your child is running on?"

You might be getting this wake-up call from me, but I got mine from a doctor a few years ago. When I first entered into parenthood, I had a full-time job and a house to take care of. It all started with a harmless cartoon episode to keep my kid busy while I worked around the house. Long before I knew it, my child was hooked on the tablet. He had to eat with it, sleep with it and even shower with it. I tried to get him off of it, but he would throw tantrums on tantrums until he got his way. Plus, if I am really honest, his screen time meant I could get a break to relax from my hectic routine. Out of love, frustration, and a chance to relax, I usually gave into him.

One day, I got a concerned call from his school that he kept dozing off in his classes and if there was a problem at home. On our way back home, to add to my worry, he complained that his eyes were burning and he had a headache. I took him to the doctor immediately, who made me realize how excessive his screen time was, and it was the reason behind everything.

Moreover, his one bad habit impacted other aspects of his life deeply. Being chained to a screen, he did not engage in much physical activity, barely had friends, and lacked behind in school. It was then when I started monitoring his habits because the smallest habit can turn into an addiction and cause irreversible damage.

Let me tell you about a small habit so you can understand the problem better. Giving your child just two minutes of brushing his teeth properly twice a day can prevent him from cavities, rotten teeth, gum diseases, and teeth aches. Now, this habit accounts for only four minutes a day, and see how much of a big impact it can make. Being a parent to two children, I understand how tricky and challenging parenthood is. Knowing what is best for your child is not always easy. Trying to incorporate new habits into your child's life is a whole other story.

After my wake-up call, I tried to figure out what other habits my kid might have that could harm his mental and physical health. To my surprise, I found many. I researched everything about habits; which one's children should have and which ones they should not. It was a lot of work, and if you have done the same, you can relate to me. If you have got through that process, you might have realized that making your children break old unhealthy habits and then try to work out new healthy habits around their routine and personality is not an easy task. Making your kids stick to the new healthy habits is something even more demanding. I have been through all of it, and I understand the overwhelming situation that you are in.

This book has been written with the complications of habit building and breaking in mind and ensuring you have a complete guide on what habits to make a part of your child's life and how you can take on this challenge.

After going through this book, you will understand the importance of parenting styles and how they can impact your child's development. This part is essential because you use one of these styles to cater to the habit-building or breaking process in your child. Moving on, you will get to know what healthy habits are, why habit building is critical at a young age, and if your child's habits are healthy.

Then you will be provided with a thorough account of healthy habits for a sound mind and body of your child. You will learn how you can smooth the habit-building process, make the good one's stick, and make the bad ones stay away.

The first two chapters of the book will build an understanding and clear concept, while the rest of the three chapters will be devoted to providing a solution to your habit issues with your child.

The reason you can look up to me on this subject is because I have two children myself and I have a degree in management and education. The knowledge of my degree helps me guide my own children and others towards a healthy lifestyle. I have been mentoring and tutoring young people, all the while giving them leadership training for two years. Experiencing parenthood has developed a passion in me for learning and teaching positive parenting strategies and nourishing families around me.

I have carefully put together every chapter and every habit in this book in a way that I know can benefit children and allow them to have a happy and fulfilling life. You do not need to browse the internet, trapped in a pool of confusing information.

This book is all you need for your habit-related troubles.

Let's begin.

Chapter 1: A Healthy Kid, a Healthy Adult

Parents perform the most significant role in their child's overall development. The development of a child's personality is dependent on parental direction. Parenting is a never-ending task. It is not something you can avoid whenever you want, because children need their parents to keep them on course all the time.

Positive parenting increases children's cognitive, social, and problem-solving abilities as they grow older. In the early years, interaction and stimulation are crucial. Children learn about being healthy, frequently exercising, developing attributes like discipline, time management, and efficient problem-solving, and eating the right foods through a play-and-learn basic routine. Parents who provide appropriate advice can instill in their children a healthy regimen that can help them attain optimal physical and mental development.

1.1 Parenting Styles and Their Impact

Parenting styles shape children's thoughts by governing their responses to stimuli. A healthy parent-child relationship is critical because it influences a child's social, emotional, physical, and attachment development, all of which influence the child's future personality, behavior, relationships, and life choices.

To put it in another way, a child's future success is built on the foundation of a parent-child relationship. In 1938, Harvard University conducted extensive research to determine how to raise successful people.

In the Harvard Grant Study, the first of its kind, 268 male Harvard undergraduates, including John F. Kennedy, were followed for the next seventy years.

Their mental and physical well-being was recorded, and their accomplishments (or lack thereof) were assessed. Researchers came to one clear conclusion: a solid relationship is a key to a happy and successful life. Having a loving and nourishing childhood is one of the best indications of adult success, well-being, and life happiness. Bowlby and Ainsworth created the Bond Theory in the 1950s, which claims that if a kid receives warm and nurturing treatment from a caregiver, he or she can build a stable bond.

If a youngster has a secure attachment, their growth and results are far more likely to be exceptional. Furthermore, the human brain is highly reliant on prior experience. The design of the brain is shaped by life events and relationships. The foundation for future mental health is laid by positive interactions with a caring and responsive parent. Childhood memories provide a source of strength that lasts forever.

Information on parenting styles is important so you can figure out what styles you lean towards and then change for the better, as you will also be using these styles for helping your child break or make habits. Let's get into it:

The Four Parenting Styles

Diana Baumrind, a psychologist, did research on over 100 preschool-aged children in the 1960s. She found certain key aspects of parenting through naturalistic observation, parental interviews, and other study approaches. Discipline tactics, communication styles, warmth and nurturing, maturity, and control expectations are among these factors. Baumrind proposed that the majority of parents have one of three parenting styles based on these dimensions.

Maccoby and Martin's later studies proposed introducing a fourth parenting style. Each of the styles has a different effect on the behavior of children:

- **Authoritarian Parenting**

   Children are expected to follow the rigorous restrictions demanded by the parents under this parenting style. Failure to observe such guidelines is frequently met with retaliation. The reasons for these rules are never explained by authoritarian parents. If pressed, the parent may simply respond, "Because I said so."

   Despite their great expectations, many parents are not very sensitive to their children. They want their children to behave admirably and avoid making mistakes, but they give very little guidance on what they should do or avoid in the future. Mistakes are punished, often harshly, but their progeny are frequently left wondering what went wrong.

   These parents, according to Baumrind, are "obedience- and status-oriented, and want their directives to be followed without question." They are frequently labeled as autocratic and overbearing.

- **Authoritative Parenting**

   An authoritative parenting style, like authoritarian parenting, establishes rules and principles for their children to follow. This parenting method, on the other hand, is far more democratic.

Authoritative parents respond to their children's queries and are willing to listen to them. Parents with this style have high expectations for their children, but they treat them with kindness, provide feedback, and provide enough support. When their children do not reach their parents' standards, they are more loving and forgiving than harsh.

According to Baumrind, "These parents should keep an eye on their children's behavior and instill clear expectations. They are aggressive, but not overbearing or confining. Rather than being punitive, their disciplinary tactics are supportive. They want their children to be aggressive as well as socially responsible, as well as self-controlled and cooperative."

Children of authoritative parents benefit from a combination of expectation and support in developing abilities like self-control, independence, and self-regulation.

- **Uninvolved Parenting**

Few demands, poor responsiveness, and limited communication describe an uninvolved parenting style. While these parents meet their children's fundamental necessities, they are often absent from their children's lives.

They may ensure that their children are fed and housed, but they provide little to no structure, guidance, rules, or even support. In other situations, these parents may even reject or ignore their children's needs.

- **Permissive Parenting**

  Permissive parents, often known as indulgent parents, place few restrictions on their children. These parents have low expectations of maturity and self-control, and that is why they rarely reprimand their children. Permissive parents, according to Baumrind, are more accommodating than demanding.

  They are unconventional and lenient, requiring no adult behavior, allowing for a great deal of self-control, and avoiding confrontation.

  Permissive parents are often loving and communicative with their children, and they frequently assume the role of a friend rather than a parent.

What Parenting Style Do You Need?

Researchers have done a variety of studies on the impact of parenting styles on children, in addition to Baumrind's first study of 100 preschool children. The following are some of the findings:

- Authoritarian parenting techniques lead to obedient and capable children, but they are less happy, socially competent, and have low self-esteem.
- Authoritative parenting techniques are likely to nurture happy, capable, and successful children.
- Permissive parenting frequently leads to children who are unhappy and lack self-control. These children are more prone to have issues with authority and have low academic performance.
- Uninvolved parenting style ranks lowest across all life domains. These kids have low self-esteem, poor self-control, and are less capable than their peers.

Authoritative parents are more likely to be perceived as rational, fair, and just and their children are more inclined to follow their parents' instructions. Furthermore, these parents provide both regulations and reasons, and children are considerably more likely to internalize their lessons.

Rather than just following the rules out of fear of punishment (as with authoritarian parents), authoritative children can know why the rules exist, realize that they are fair and appropriate, and attempt to follow them to satisfy their own internalized sense of right and wrong.

Let's also discuss some common mistakes parents need to avoid, which can make the habit-building process more complicated for your child.

1.2 Common Parenting Mistakes

Parents frequently depend only on their "parenting instincts" and fail to seek help for common parenting concerns and problems. Unfortunately, many of us do not have a natural feel for what to do in every situation we find ourselves in as parents, and we all make mistakes from time to time.

Learning how to avoid these common parenting mistakes will help you become a more effective parent while helping your kids pick good habits and leave bad ones behind:

- **Not Exhibiting Model Behavior**

   A parent can have the best advice in the world for their children, like how to behave when they are upset, how to treat others, and sincerely request them to eat their vegetables, but it is ineffective if parents simply instruct their children to do these things rather than demonstrating it via their own actions.

Unfortunately, children tend to imitate their parents' actions rather than listening to what they say. If parents want their children to engage in beneficial behaviors like treating people with kindness, they should set an example.

- **Making up Lies**

I was once sitting with a couple and their two-year-old daughter at a restaurant. Because she had removed her shoes and tossed them on the floor, her father asked her to put them back on as we were leaving, "because here there are spiders all over the floor and they will crawl into your shoes."

What a ludicrous story to scare your youngster with! If I were their daughter, I would have nightmares of the restaurant with hundreds of spiders scurrying over the floor.

It was easier for the parents to lie to their daughter than to tell her the basic truth: we have to wear our shoes at restaurants because it is the rule. They decided to lie about imaginary spiders rather than enforcing some discipline on their child.

Kids interpret what you say literally, so if you tell them lies like spiders on the floor ready to burrow into your shoes, that image will stay with them for years. They may get resentful if they learn the facts later in life.

I am not saying you have to tell your two-year-old the whole truth all of the time, but do not lie to him. They trust you.

- **Not Acknowledging Good Behavior**

Many parents make the mistake of nagging, whining, and criticizing their children, then saying nothing when they do the right thing just because they "expect" it. We get more of what we pay attention to. Parents would do a lot better if they paid attention to their children when they did the right thing and noted every little thing, they did that was correct, showed a positive attitude, put forth a little effort, or made modest progress. It would also be preferable if they did not comment on the negative aspects of their behavior and instead focused on the positive aspects. Parents who do this will find that their children are more motivated to do the right thing and are more willing to comply with their parents.

- **Realizing What is Not Working**

  It is almost as bad as not trying to address problems in the first place if you do not recognize or change your parenting tactics that are not working. Is what you are doing effective? For example, you may believe that scolding is an effective discipline strategy, but if you have to apply it every day to fix the same behavior or problem, it is not. Alternatively, if your child's bedtime routine means your child constantly getting out of bed, lasts an hour, and leaves you exhausted and your child exhausted the next morning, you will need to explore a new method to assist your child in going to bed.

- **Fighting Back**

  Fighting back causes you to become stuck in negative communication patterns. I am not talking about physically fighting with your child, but you can fight back by yelling, getting angry, or repeating yourself over and over again.

  Arguing or fighting with your children attracts unwanted attention and gives them a lot of control over you because they can get such powerful responses from you.

Fighting back will unintentionally encourage the conduct you are trying to curb rather than stopping harmful habits.

Rather than fighting back, you can do better by putting an end to power struggles and adopting more effective discipline tactics, such as time-out and applying logical consequences, rather than wasting time fighting before actually implementing them.

- **Making Idle Threats**

It is extremely aggravating when parents make threats to get their children to behave but then fail to follow through. "If you do that again, I am turning the car around and we are going back home," or "If you keep doing that, I am sending you to bed," are common instances. The youngster then misbehaves again, and the threat is not followed through on.

Children are not foolish. They pick up quickly, and if you make a threat and then ignore it, they will stop believing anything you say in the future. If your child is misbehaving and you tell them, "Do that one more time and you are going to bed," follow through and send them to bed.

This is an easy lesson to remember, and a youngster who has previously been disciplined is much more likely to listen to you the following time.

- **Setting Unrealistic Expectations**

  It is natural for parents to have expectations for their children. You must, however, carefully assess each of your child's capabilities. Examine whether the goals you are setting are realistic and attainable for them. Keep in mind that if you have two or more children, each one has their own personality and different ability to satisfy those demands.

- **Tricking Your Kids**

  I once read a story that a woman was frustrated by her toddler's constant desire to eat off her plate. She once placed her child's food on her plate so that he would eat it as if it were his own.

  He did not throw a tantrum because he ate his own food. No, it is not right. According to her son, his mother appeared to be smiling and pleased that her son was eating off her plate. She taught him that eating her food is fine because that is exactly what he was doing.

It is easy to be tempted to 'trick' your child in order to get them to do what you want, like in the example above. Even if the conclusion is what you want, making them believe they are doing something wrong is a horrible lesson. Make and follow the rules instead. It could have been better for the mother in the long run if she had taught her son that eating food out of others' plates is wrong.

These are a few mistakes you absolutely need to keep away from while teaching your child the right habits. Let's now study what healthy brain and body habits are and why they are important for your child's development.

Chapter 2: The "What," " How" and "Why" of Healthy Habits

People do not make decisions about their future; instead, they make decisions about their habits, and their habits make decisions about their future. This holds true in marriage, parenting, healthcare, business, and many aspects of life. Habits are extremely important—-far more so than we may realize. Our minds adhere to routines to the detriment of all else, including common sense. Over time, these habits become stronger and stronger. They really trigger neurological urges that feed into a habit cycle. There is a trigger that sets off a habit that rewards us by releasing pleasure chemicals in the brain. This habit loop repeats itself, eventually becoming automatic. We should better double-check that they are the appropriate ones. And here is the scary part: when a habit forms, the brain ceases to participate completely in decision-making. Habits clearly define who you are. Routines become so ingrained in your life that they eventually start to define you. You may, however, alter your habits. The new ones will follow the same pattern as the previous ones: steady repetition. These habits will provide the groundwork for the rest of your life.

If you choose the habits that make you happy, you will be a happy person. You have the ability to pick the type of life you want to live.

Habits are beneficial because they allow you to spend your energy on other things. However, unless you actively combat a harmful habit and replace it with other routines, the behavior will repeat itself whenever a trigger occurs. All habits can be replaced or changed, but it is not easy because habits are never truly gone; they are only replaced by new ones. Let me tell you more about habits in a bit more detail.

2.1 The "What" and "How" Part of It

Habits are the minor decisions and activities you take on a daily basis. Your behaviors are effectively the sum of your life today. What you do on a daily basis (i.e., what you spend your time thinking about and doing) shapes the person you are, the beliefs you hold, and the character you project. Better habits start with better habits, from procrastination to productivity to strength and nutrition. A habit is a learned activity that gradually becomes reflexive. A certain situation is frequently responsible for the conduct. As part of your morning ritual, you could automatically clean your teeth after finishing breakfast.

A habit might be beneficial, harmful, or neutral. Meditating or stretching for ten minutes a day when you are worried are also good habits to develop. Texting while driving or biting your nails are two examples of bad habits. Having the same brand of cereal every morning or traveling the same route to work is examples of neutral habits.

Why do we need habits?

Brain Efficacy

Our brain uses habits to improve its efficiency. Our brain converts daily actions and behaviors into habits, allowing us to perform them automatically and without much effort, freeing up our mental resources for more essential tasks.

Our brain's plan has a lot of advantages for us. It enables us to work more effectively in our daily lives. Can you think what it would be like if you had to consider and ponder over every single activity or response? We would be unable to do anything but think.

If you have ever done something for the first time, you will recall that it took a lot of concentration and brainpower. However, as you practiced them, it grew easier. The mental strength required to do these tasks has greatly diminished. This is known as "chunking," and it is the foundation of habits. We unconsciously rely on these "chunks" of behavior every day.

The brain is always in the process of acquiring information and guiding human behavior appropriately. It makes no difference whether or not consciousness is involved in the decision-making process, and most of the time, it is not.

The majority of habits begin as deliberate, goal-oriented activities. For example, parents may ask a child to wash their hands before eating. The child may just wash their hands to receive praise from a parent at first. Before each meal, they may require reminders to complete the chore. However, once the washing habit is repeated, the youngster will become accustomed to it and will no longer require reminders. Whether or not the parent encourages the behavior, they will wash their hands before eating. Because the action is motivated more by context than a particular incentive, it can be classified as a habit at this point.

The act of washing one's hands before meals takes a number of steps at the start of the procedure. The youngster should proceed to the sink, turn on the water, lather themselves with soap, and dry their hands. However, when the habit develops, the brain tends to link these processes together as a single "chunk." In other words, it begins to see a four-step procedure as a single act of handwashing.

How are Habits Formed?

In 1990s, a group of researchers found a brain process that is at the heart of every habit. This basic three-step loop is extremely effective because it is hard-wired into our brain. To change habits, you must understand

- Any **trigger** that informs your brain when and which habit to use is referred to as a cue.
- A **routine** is an activity, feeling, or behavior that is repeated.
- Your brain uses **reward** to determine whether or not a loop is advantageous to you.

In the hand washing example, the cue is the parent asking the child to wash hands before eating. The routine is washing hands. The reward is the praise or approval of parents.

Let me quote another example. Consider this scenario: You are bored, which is a cue. You reach for a bottle of sugary cold drink as the routine. You feel comfortable and joyful as a result, and that is the reward.

The cue and the reward have a significant impact on habit formation. It causes cravings and causes you to repeat certain habits or acts. You must replace the looping process with something else that provides the same reward to break a habit.

How can you Break Your Child's Bad Habits?

If you believe that it is time to assist your child in breaking a habit, follow these steps:

- Explain why you do not like the habit. This method can be used with children as young as three or four years old to help raise awareness of the situation. Something along the lines of, "When you bite your nails, it bothers me. It does not appear to be attractive. Could you perhaps refrain from doing so?" Most importantly, do not chastise or lecture the next time you notice someone gnawing their nails. Punishment, ridicule, or criticism may lead to an increase in the undesirable conduct.

- Involve your child in the habit-breaking process. If your 5-year-old comes home from kindergarten crying because the other kids teased him about his thumb sucking, see it as a request for assistance. Parents can inquire as to what their children believe they could do to break the habit or whether they desire to break the habit. Come up with some ideas for how you and your partner can work together to break the bad habit.

- Alternative habits should be suggested. If your youngster bites his nails, for example, instead of saying, "Do not bite your nails," say, "Let's wiggle our fingers." It will help him become more aware of the behavior and may also serve as a reminder. Provide a distraction, such as helping you in the kitchen or working on a craft, to keep your child's attention occupied.

- Self-control should be rewarded and praised. Allow your child girl to wear nail polish, for example, if she allows her nails to grow. Alternatively, whenever your son refrains from sucking his thumb, praise him and reward him with a sticker or other little prize.

- Reward good behavior in a consistent manner. If you do not pay attention to positive behavior, it will fade away over time. Before the old habit disappears, the new, positive one must be firmly formed.

It is critical that children be motivated to stop the habit in order to achieve the best results. Habits take time to form, so it will take time for them to be replaced by new behaviors. You need to be patient. Now let's move forward with the understanding of why all this fuss is important.

2.2 The "Why" Part of It

Children are affected deeply by their surroundings. When it comes to teaching children habits, it is crucial to start early, especially since children acquire habits by the age of nine. It can be difficult to break both bad and good habits.

The earlier we start teaching good habits, the more likely they are to stick for years.

Here are some points for further elaboration:

- **Be Mindful of Their Formative Years**

  Take advantage of your child's formative years to teach them the most vital behaviors and to ensure that they will continue these habits as they grow older. Do not wait until you are sure your child understands what you are saying. They mostly process and pick up on more than we realize.

Take, for example, hand washing. It is a simple habit to instill at a young age. Set a good example by emphasizing how you wash your hands since you realize how vital it is.

Children can be taught the habit by reminding them of how often they wash their hands. Invite them to join you in singing a poem to ensure that you have cleaned your hands thoroughly. This turns the practice into a game, allowing children to associate handwashing with sentiments of enjoyment and happiness.

When your child has mastered hand washing, you can begin to teach them when they should wash their hands, such as before eating, after playing, after sneezing or coughing, and after using the restroom.

- **Equip Them with Self Control**

  It is challenging to make the best judgments all of the time, even as grownups. Consider how challenging it must be for a child to choose healthy food over sweet temptations.

  It is quite tempting to dismiss this as a problem, but children who acquire self-control at a young age have more chances to succeed later in life. It is critical to lead by example and assist children in developing self-control while they are still young.

Teach kids about good eating habits and how to get more fruits and veggies into their diets. Make dinnertime a time for family connection. As you prepare dinner, assign age-appropriate responsibilities to your children to assist you in the kitchen.

Make healthful snacks accessible to children as well. Sugary sweets are convenient to grab on the go, which is one of the reasons children choose them. Healthy eating is more convenient and enticing, with pre-sliced veggies and fruit in snack-sized containers in the fridge that the kids can reach.

There are also numerous children's books available that may teach your children about healthy eating habits, as well as other beneficial practices. Make a day of it by going to the library and collecting such books.

- **Give Them Less Bad Habits to Break Later On**

   Habits are unconsciously performed acts and behaviors that are extremely difficult to quit. This is because the chemical dopamine is released into the brain when we form and repeat habits, resulting in a pleasurable feeling and a strong habit. This is why it is critical for your children to start developing healthy habits at a young age.

There are many questionnaires on the internet that can help you determine how healthy your child's habits are. In the next two chapters, we will thoroughly study the habits absolutely essential for a child's healthy body and mind development.

Chapter 3: Healthy Habits for a Happy Mind

The most important thing to keep in mind is that you are a role model for your child. Your habits have an impact on the habits of your children. If you have harmful behaviors, such as expressing emotions inappropriately, communicating poorly, or always expecting the worst, your child is more likely to adopt them. If you have healthy behaviors, like eating a balanced diet, exercising regularly, and looking forward to tomorrow, your children are more likely to develop those habits in their own life.

Good mental habits help you enjoy life and cope with challenges. It offers a feeling of inner strength and well-being. With that in mind, let's discuss some habits which will favor your child's healthy mental development.

3.1 Active Communication

The capacity to communicate effectively is an important life skill for children in the twenty-first century. The better we are at this skill, the better our lives will be. The ability to convey ourselves effectively and confidently in all parts and areas of our lives is referred to as communication skills. Communication is the process of passing information to others and comprehending what is communicated to us, resulting in a greater level of understanding among individuals. In many instances, good communication skills may provide better understanding among persons, reduce tensions, and create a peaceful atmosphere.

Children begin communicating with their moms from the time they are born, letting them know they have come through their first cry.

Later in life, children must learn how to communicate in order to fully comprehend human society, to communicate their ideas to others around them, and to understand what knowledge others wish to express to them.

In humans, there are three basic modes of communication: verbal (with words), nonverbal (without speech but with gestures), and visual. They include a variety of other abilities, such as observing, listening, and speaking.

The following are some fun activities for kids to build good communication habits:

- **The Telephone Game**

This popular and entertaining game helps child improve their listening skills and may be enjoyed by children of all ages. Other family members can be included as well. Everyone should sit in a circle, close enough to whisper easily. Start the game with one child whispering a message into the ear of the player sitting next to him, who then whispers it into the ears of the person next to him, and until everyone in the circle has a turn. In the end, the message can be revealed by the last person who received it. The original message and the final message received are very certainly going to be different. Begin with a simple message and work your way up to more complicated ones.

- **Giving Directions**

This simple game can be used as a nonverbal communication activity for children. Ask your child to jot down directions to his favorite store or park in the area. Then, go to the location with your child, following the stated directions. Along the way, assist him in understanding how he may improve them or things he might mention to improve communication.

- **Giving Presentation**

  This engaging practice will not only help your child improve his oral language skills but will also help him become more comfortable speaking in public. You can suggest a variety of topics, ranging from reciting a favorite poem to expressing his thoughts on contemporary issues such as water conservation, recycling, and the use of technology, among others. Request him to prepare a short presentation to give at a family gathering, a local park event, or anywhere else he feels at ease.

- **Show and Tell**

  This activity can be a fun way for kids to practice verbal communication. Give your child a topic, such as his favorite book, favorite fruit, or a family road trip. Ask him to display an item relating to the issue and talk five lines about it. This practice can help your child gain confidence, expand their vocabulary, and improve their eloquence.

- **Impromptu Speech**

  Extempore speech, often known as spontaneous speech, is an important aspect of oral communication and can be utilized to improve communication abilities.

Extempore assists your child in thinking on his feet and correctly conveying his ideas. This activity will also adequately prepare him for future employment opportunities. Make cards on interesting topics, and have your child pick one and speak about it for a few minutes spontaneously.

3.2 Time Management

If you believe adults are the only ones who have to cope with the morning rush, you are mistaken. Even children feel pressurized by words such as "you are going to be late for school!" or as "you need to get dressed quickly!"

Even though young children have a limited understanding of time, it is never too early to teach them time management skills. Not only is this an excellent opportunity for parents to educate their children on how to tell time, but it also teaches them how to plan their schedules autonomously, which is critical to their future academic success. Follow the steps below for building this valuable habit.

- **Family Calendar**

Family calendars serve as a road map for everyone's commitments in your home. With a quick glance, you can see that one of your children has basketball on Tuesday, scouts on Monday, and karate and gymnastics on Wednesday.

The entire family should contribute to the creation of a single document that keeps everyone on track. Banner paper is ideal for family calendars because it can be sketched on, colored on, or painted on. Make it a family art project so that everyone knows who has what obligations on what days. Color-code your calendar so that each person's schedule is a different color. This simple activity allows kids to see days at a time in one spot. Another advantage is that you may use your preparation time to maximize family time together.

- **Individual Calendar**

Each child should have his own calendar in addition to the family calendar. That way, he can keep his own timetable in his room that is more precise for his specific needs than the family calendar.

Break down the tasks for the day or week on this calendar. Encourage your children to use their personal calendars to add new tasks and to check off those that have been completed. This might include everything from how to prepare for a soccer match to what projects he needs to finish before the science fair.

- **Routine into Checklist**

  This is the best practice you can do during the week to relieve family tension. During the school year, most children follow a similar daily routine—showering, dressing, and so on. Rather than nagging your children to complete tasks, communicate with them and design a checklist that includes personal care and age-appropriate chores. Hold them accountable for completing their assignments. Send them to the chart whenever you hear "but I did not know!" or "what should I do now!" There will be no more excuses.

- **Measuring Time**

  Even children who can tell the time do not always know how to measure it. Set a timer for a chunk of time when they are meant to be doing a task to assist them. Keep a clock nearby and offer them a vocal countdown as the minutes pass so they can develop a sense of how long these chunks are. You are not aiming to instill in your children the habit of keeping time. Your goal is to simply assist them in grasping the concept of an hour, 15 minutes, or even five minutes.

They will understand the next time you say, "We are leaving in five minutes," that you do not imply they have time to watch TV, play with their toys, or clean their room first.

- **Stay Time Focused**

   When the kids are getting along so well, it is tempting to give them a few additional minutes of playtime. Alternatively, there are days when you want the kids to spend extra time studying, despite the fact that your time management plan requires them to begin getting ready for bed at 7:00 p.m.

   Stay on task while your children are still learning about time management. When the timer goes off, no matter how invested they are in the current task, move on to the next one on their checklist. Even if it is only for a few minutes, deviating from the timetable might throw kids off. Stick to your routine, especially in the first few days and weeks of learning how to manage your time.

- **Time Management Tools**

Incorporate kid-friendly time management tools in your child's life, from apps to colorful magnetic calendars. The idea is to use graphics and strategies that your children will understand. You are the only person who understands what will work best for each of your child's learning styles.

Apps may appeal to children who enjoy using technology. Magnetic calendars for kids allow your children to arrange their days visually using colorful magnets for everything from sports practices to vacations. You can always get crafty and develop your own time management tools to fit your family's routine.

- **Be a Coach**

Consider shifting your mindset from being your children's manager to being their coach. You hound your kids to get tasks completed because you are the manager, and you are responsible for the outcome. Everyone digs in their heels at this point, and a power battle develops.

Instead, as a coach, you can serve as a kind outsider who offers advice and support. You empower your children with knowledge, then stand back and let them make their own decisions, good or bad. It is freeing for everyone and fosters long-term self-confidence in children.

- **Make it Fun**

  Learning time management should, however, be enjoyable for children. Make your calendars using crayons. Stickers can be used to commemorate significant occasions. Make it a contest to see who can finish simple household duties that normally take a long time, such as putting on their shoes, cleaning their teeth, or getting their backpacks ready for school the next day. The more enjoyable you make time management for your children, the easier it will be for them to grasp the value of time and how to manage that never-ending clock.

3.3 Discipline and Self Control

The main goal of any parenting technique should be to teach your young one's self-control, regardless of the form of discipline you apply.

Self-discipline enables children to resist unhealthy urges, postpone satisfaction, and bear the discomfort required to achieve long-term objectives. Self-discipline is essential to helping youngsters become responsible people, whether it is choosing to switch off the TV to do homework or rejecting an extra cookie while Dad is not looking. Let me tell you how you can help your child with self-discipline and self-control:

- **Give Them Structure**

Like I advised in the above section, create the same schedule for your child every day, and he will become accustomed to it. They will be less inclined to get sidetracked by other activities if they know what they are required to do.

An ideal morning routine allows children to recognize when it is time to brush their teeth, eat breakfast, comb their hair, and dress. An ideal after-school schedule teaches children how to balance homework, chores, and relaxing activities. A healthy bedtime routine will also assist children in settling down and falling asleep sooner.

- **Give Them Reasons**

While teaching your child how to make good decisions, an authoritative parenting style is ideal, since it can help him grasp why the rules exist. Explain, "Do your homework first and then having free time later as a prize for getting your homework done is a smart choice." This aids children in comprehending the rationale for your regulations. Instead of stating, "My mother told me I had to do this." In this way, your child will realize the rules are there for a reason.

A brief explanation of why you believe certain options are important can assist your child in understanding his choices better.

- **Give Them Consequences**

Natural consequences can sometimes convey life's most important lessons. A kid who consistently forgets to take their coat as they rush out the door will not learn if their coat is delivered to school by their parents. Experiencing the consequences of his actions naturally (like being cold) may encourage the kid to remember to bring his coat the next time.

Kids require logical consequences at other times. When a kid who is too careless with their computer, loses computer privileges, they may learn to be nicer. Alternatively, a youngster who has difficulty getting out of bed in the morning may require getting into bed earlier.

It is critical to stay away from power struggles. Forcing your youngster to accomplish anything will not teach him or her self-discipline.

Describe to your youngster what will happen if he or she makes a terrible decision. After that, let your youngster make the decision. "If you pick up your mess, you can have more time to play outside," you might say. If they do not pick up, go ahead with a consequence, but do not try to force them to comply or yell.

Remember that children must learn to make good decisions for themselves by considering the repercussions of their actions.

- **Praise Them**

When your youngster shows self-control, give him or her praise and positive attention. Make a point of highlighting the positive conduct you would like to see more of. For instance, in place of "I appreciate not striking your sister when you were upset," use "I appreciate you for using your words for solving the matter."

It is fairly common for good behavior to go unrecognized. Praise for good decisions raises the chances that the child will repeat the action.

When your children accomplish something without needing to be reminded, give them praise. "Way to sit down and finish your schoolwork before I even asked you." or "I am very proud of you for cleaning and organizing your room all by yourself today!" Even compliments like, "Wow, you did a great job placing your plate in the sink after you finished eating," can motivate repeated actions.

- **Take it Step by Step**

  Self-discipline is a long-term process that requires years to perfect. To modify behavior one step at a time, use age-friendly disciplining tactics.

  You can use a chart on the wall stating to comb hair, brush teeth, and get dressed. Do not expect them to execute the entire morning routine without any help or reminders.

  Remind your child to look at the wall chart as needed until he is able to complete each job independently. They will eventually require lesser reminders, and the chart will be obsolete.

  Guide your child to acquire a new skill or develop more independence in one tiny step at a time when possible.

- **Give Them Rewards**

  A reward structure can be used to address certain behavioral issues. The basic concept of a token system is that a child earns a set number of tokens by engaging in desired behaviors (referred to as "target behaviors"), which they can then exchange – effectively using them as currency – for television time, special foods, passes, or other prizes.

  A token economy system may benefit an older child who has trouble completing homework and chores on time. A sticker chart that is same token economy might help inspire a preschooler who has trouble staying in their own room at night.

  Short-term reward mechanisms should be used. As your child develops self-control, gradually remove them.

  Remember that there are several non-monetary incentives. Extra privileges, such as electronics time, might be used to encourage your youngster to be more responsible.

3.4 Emotional Intelligence

The essential childrearing responsibility you have as a parent is to teach your children to respect emotion. Emotional intelligence or EQ can be defined as a person's capacity to correctly express and control emotions while also respecting the sentiments of others. It is a collection of abilities that may be learned by children at any age. Your children are much more likely to have excellent mental health, secure life, meaningful relationships, and a rewarding income source if you and your partner treat each other and the children with emotional awareness and empathy. Here are a few basic parenting techniques that will help your child develop emotional intelligence:

- **Identifying Emotions**

One of the best signs of how someone is feeling is their facial expressions and body language. Recognizing these signs, however, may not come naturally. Taking the time to teach these visual clues can go a long way toward improving a child's ability to relate to oneself and others.

Playing emotion charades with your kids is like slipping greens into your child's breakfast smoothie. This is how you can play it:

➢ **Act 1**: This focuses on your feelings about certain topics. For example, how does your child react when you say, "Let's go grab some ice cream?"

➢ **Act 2:** Write down a scene that would make someone pleased, terrified, furious, or any other emotion on a piece of paper. Fold the strips and place them in a container or bag. After that, have family members pick a strip to act out.

➢ **Act 3:** You will concentrate on expanding your child's emotional language in the second version. How many different ways can you express anger? What about words for happiness?

➢ **Act 4:** Write down synonyms for the words happy, angry, sad, scared, etc., on a strip of paper and act them out.

- **Healthy Expression of Emotions**

    Kids must learn that just because they are furious, they do not have the right to hit someone. Teach your youngster how to deal with difficult emotions early on. Encourage your child to take a break for himself or herself. When they are agitated, tell them to go to their room or another peaceful spot. This may assist them in calming down before breaking a rule and being sent to timeout.

Teach your youngster good coping mechanisms for sad feelings. If your child is angry or sad because a friend refuses to play with him, talk to him about how he can cope with his feelings. When children are unsure what to do when they are upset, they often turn angry or engage in attention-seeking activities. You can also use these two activities:

> Statements that begin with the phrase "I feel..." While speaking to children, this is a favorite. Using "I feel" statements keep the discourse open, neutral, and caring. There are fewer instances of ranting, blame, and damaged feelings.

> Practice breathing exercises together. Breathing in and breathing out can help us regain our equilibrium and serenity.

- **Positive Reinforcement**

Positive consequences should be used to reinforce good behavior. Praise your child for expressing his feelings in a socially acceptable manner, such as "I really appreciate the way you used your words to tell your brother you were upset at him."

- **Model Behavior**

  Children are prone to imitate the behaviors they observe. This is why practicing emotional literacy is one of the most effective ways to teach it. If you ask your child to use his words when he is upset, but he sees you throw your phone after a missed call, your words are not going to work. Demonstrate healthy coping mechanisms for difficult emotions.

  Identify and express occasions when you are upset or frustrated. "Oh no, that car just pulled in front of me," you might say. Then take a few calm breaths or demonstrate another healthy coping technique so that your child can learn to recognize the strategies you employ when you are angry.

3.5 Problem Solving and Creative Thinking

Whether your child cannot find his math assignment or has forgotten his or her lunch, good problem-solving abilities are essential for them to manage their lives. According to a study published in Behavior Research and Therapy, children who lack problem-solving skills are more likely to experience despair and suicidality. Furthermore, the researchers discovered that teaching problem-solving abilities to a youngster can boost mental health.

You can start teaching your child basic problem-solving abilities in preschool and continue to assist them in developing their talents throughout high school and beyond.

Kids who are overwhelmed or despondent are less likely to try to solve an issue. They will feel more secure in their capacity to try if you provide them a clear formula for addressing challenges. The steps to teaching problem solving are as follows:

- **Identifying Problem**

  For kids who are stuck, simply articulating the situation out loud can make a tremendous difference. "You do not have someone to play with at recess," or "You are not sure if you should take the advanced math class," are examples of how you might help your child explain the problem.

- **Brainstorm Solutions**

  Create a list of potential solutions to the problem. It is important to emphasize that all of the answers do not have to be good (at least not at this point). If your child cannot think of any idea, assist them in finding a solution.

Even the most ridiculous answer or far-fetched concept can be a solution. The idea is to show them that with a little imagination, they can come up with a variety of possible answers.

- **Identify Pros and Cons**

  Assist your child in identifying the positive and negative aspects of each prospective solution.

- **Decide on a Solution**

  Encourage your youngster to choose a solution once they have considered the good and negative outcomes.

- **Test the Solution**

  Ask them to try a solution and see what happens. They can always attempt another solution from the list they created in step two if it does not work out.

Do not rush to address your child's problems for them when they arise. Instead, assist them in completing the problem-solving processes. When they need help, provide it, but also encourage them to handle challenges on their own. If they cannot come up with ideas, step in and assist them. But do not help them by telling them what to do right away.

Use a problem-solving strategy when dealing with behavioral challenges. Take a seat together and explain, "You have been having trouble finishing your assignments recently. Let's work together to fix this issue." You may still need to discipline misbehavior, but make it obvious that you are committed to finding a solution so they can do better next time.

"What can we do to make sure that this does not happen again?" ask them if they have forgotten to bring their soccer cleats to practice. Wait for them to come up with their own solutions.

Kids come up with creative solutions. "I will write a note and post it on my door to remind me to pack them before I go," they might say, or "I will pack my bag the night before and make a checklist to remind me what has to go in my bag". When your child is practicing their problem-solving skills, praise them. Natural consequences may also aid in the development of problem-solving abilities. Just double-check that it is safe to do so. For example, allow your teenager to spend all of their money during the first 10 minutes of your visit to an amusement park. Then, without spending any money, let them go for the remainder of the day.

Later have a conversation about problem-solving and how to make better decisions in the future. Consider these natural outcomes as an opportunity to teach others about problem-solving.

3.6 Effective Learning

Given that most children are unlikely to become enamored of homework and studying anytime soon, what can we really do to assist them?

It takes a healthy set of habits to do well in school, regardless of grade. It also necessitates determination and perseverance. These skills could even help kids deal with all of life's duties and obstacles. Instilling the following study habits in our children is an excellent place to start if we want them to be self-motivated for success:

- **No Distractions**

We understand that one of the most serious issues with homework is not our children's inability to complete it. It is the avoidance that is the problem. While there might be different reasons for this avoidance, we can overcome it by eliminating distractions.

It may seem apparent, but in these technologically saturated families, removing distractions like iPads, cell phones, and television is becoming increasingly difficult. However, the more we do so during study hours, the more our kids will be able to focus on the work at hand.

- **Homework is Fun**

The most typical reason for homework avoidance is that it is perceived as a burden. After a long day at school, it is understandable that it is the last thing on their minds. They simply want to unwind or play. Nonetheless, homework must be completed.

Instill the notion that homework may be enjoyable whenever feasible or, at least, that it has the potential to be intriguing. You are most likely wondering how you are going to make thirty math equations even remotely interesting or enjoyable. Especially when children inquire, "When will I ever apply this in real life?" This is really pointless. Consider linking school lessons with family activities to give them a dose of realism. Perhaps your second-grader is doing research for a book report on food groups.

She can assist in the planning of that night's dinner menu while she learns each food group. She may proudly explain what she has learned later while serving the family an unusual dinner that represents the food groups — and their rainbow of colors.

If your high school kid dreads his science project but is a huge Star Wars fan, assist him to come up with project ideas that appeal to his passion, such as the concept of traveling at light speed, which he can then enrich with his favorite characters and tales from the franchise.

Math can lead to a lot of intriguing, real-life examples, e.g., math helps you make buildings, so try to promote some creativity while your kids are merely staring at numbers.

Being creative may take more time on our part, but we will save it for when they are interested enough to participate and begin imagining on their own.

- **Self-Learning**

Many of us have developed the habit of assisting our children with their schoolwork, often to the point of tiredness. After all, we get worried.

The basic truth is that children must do their own job. They must see how devoting time to comprehending and completing a task may pay off. They must feel empowered by the fact that they earned a good mark on their Solar System project through their own efforts, not through parental assistance (or nagging). Sure, we may guide, encourage, review work, and educate our children on how to manage their homework, but they must put up the greatest effort.

- **Embracing Failure**

  When children complete their homework and study on their own, they are more likely to make mistakes, fail examinations, and receive poor grades, all of which can be tough for us to accept and see.

  In our society, accepting—even encouraging—failure is becoming more difficult. We are concentrating on winning the competition. Allowing our children to make mistakes and turn incorrect responses into learning opportunities, on the other hand, is a vital life skill. Reviewing our children's schoolwork with them is a terrific opportunity to recognize their efforts while also keeping a lookout for any problems they may be experiencing.

If we choose to do so, we must remember to focus on the effort put forth in the task rather than the mistakes they may have made. We need to praise them for their achievements.

3.7 Being Constructive in Teamwork

Teamwork is a sought-after skill in the business since it fosters empathy and improves learning capacities. However, today's tech-savvy kids are typically more concerned with their own efforts than with collaboration. According to a Pew Research Center survey, teamwork is one of the most crucial qualities youngsters need to succeed in today's world. How can you develop this habit in your kids? Let me answer:

- **Organized Activities**

  Especially if your child comes from a single-child household, enrolling them in an extracurricular activity that requires group participation is a terrific approach to teach them the value of teamwork. The trick is to enroll your children in an activity that matches their interests. Team sports, chess club, scouts, yearbook committee and volunteer work are all excellent examples.

- **Group Bonding and Socializing**

  There are many activities and games that may be used to foster teamwork in a group setting, but the key is to keep the activities both enjoyable and discrete. If you say the words "teamwork activity," you will undoubtedly hear protests from older students who do not want to play an organized game.

  For playdates, celebrations, or other activities, parents can organize some of these teamwork-based games aimed at all age groups:

  - High schoolers: Egg Drop
  - Middle schoolers: Who Am I
  - Elementary schoolers: Scavenger Hunt
  - Preschoolers: Follow the Leader

- **Positive Examples**

  Kids' heroes and mentors are frequently found in the television series they watch, so it is critical to fill their limited screen time with programs that teach vital character traits.

- **Encouraging Peers**

  Teamwork is built by teaching children to look outside of their individual bubbles and see the needs of others. Encourage your children to support their teammates at sporting events, congratulate their classmates on their academic achievements, and inquire about the key life events from their peers.

- **Being Co-operative at Home**

  Parents understand that teaching opportunities begin in their own homes. Thus the family should place a strong focus on teamwork. Teach and demonstrate to your children that a happy home is built by everyone's cooperation. Give your children home jobs, ask them to assist their siblings or grandparents, and reward them when they try to work with others.

These were the seven habits emphasizing mental capabilities and health for a fruitful and mature lifestyle. We will move forward with healthy habits for the body.

Chapter 4: Healthy Habits for a Happy Body

A good defense is a good offense. Long-term health is the outcome of a good defense — preventative, proactive, and healthful choices that affect our health today, tomorrow, and in the future. We must begin by being a healthy, vital younger person if we want to be a healthy, vital older person.

Good health is not an accident. It is the consequence of a lifetime of healthy practices. You can ensure that you not only live longer but also live well by developing healthy habits now. To maintain your kid's physical and emotional health as he ages, he must first alter the simple decisions he makes on a daily basis. Let's begin with some habits you need for a healthy body.

4.1 Healthy Nutritious Eating

Getting your children to eat healthily might be difficult due to peer pressure and junk food advertising on television. When you consider your own hectic schedule, it is no surprise that many children's diets are based on takeout and convenience. However, starting a healthy diet can have a significant impact on your child's health, assisting them in maintaining a healthy weight, stabilizing their emotions, sharpening their minds, and avoiding a number of health issues.

A balanced diet can also improve your child's mental and emotional well-being, reducing the risk of mental and emotional disorders like anxiety, depression, bipolar disorder, ADHD, and schizophrenia.

Remember that your children are not born with a taste for pizza and French fries and a dislike for broccoli and carrots. As adolescents are exposed to unhealthier food options, this conditioning takes place over time. It is, however, feasible to retrain your children's eating habits so that they prefer healthier meals.

The earlier you introduce good, nutritious foods into a child's diet, the easier it will be for them to form a long-term healthy relationship with food. It is also possible that it will be easier and take less time than you think. You can teach healthy eating habits to your children without making mealtimes a battleground, giving them the best chance to develop into well-balanced, healthy people.

- **Grocery Shopping with Kids**

Bringing kids inside the supermarket can make them more excited about the meals and snacks to come because they will have some input. When possible, include children in meal planning and preparation.

Picking different colors of fruits and vegetables can be made into a game (green, yellow and red peppers, broccoli, and orange carrots.) Then, speak about what recipes you can cook with your rainbow of vegetables in the coming week, such as a stir-fry. Asking children to choose recipes or dishes that they would like to help buy and prepare can be an exciting way to get them interested in cooking (and eating.)

- **Urge Them to be Adventurous**

One of the biggest presents you can offer your children is to teach them to appreciate a variety of flavors other than sugar and salt.

Do not give up on the first try; a child may need to try anything up to ten times before they appreciate it. Encouraging your children that trying new foods is a sign that they are maturing, is a wonderful strategy. Praise them for trying new meals, even if they do not finish them.

Encourage children to try the samples at the supermarket or deli — if it is fun and exciting, kids will try anything. Take them grocery shopping and let them select a fresh meal. Serve it alongside meals they already enjoy, and they will likely enjoy the new dish as well.

- **Eat Together**

  For both parents and children, family meals are a soothing practice. Family meals provide predictability for children, as well as an opportunity for parents to catch up with their children. According to studies, families who eat meals together have higher-quality diets that include more vegetables and fruits and less sugary beverages and fast food.

  You can try serving the same dishes to everyone at mealtimes to help even the pickiest eaters develop their palates. Do not be concerned if your youngster still refuses to eat something. It can take a few tries for her to eat it.

  You could also consider the following suggestions:

  > Allow your children to invite a friend to dinner.

  > Involve your child in meal preparation and planning.

  > Maintain a relaxed and amicable atmosphere throughout dinner by refraining from lecturing or arguing.

  Make an effort to provide nutritional meals and a time when everyone can attend. To accommodate a kid who is at sports practice, this could entail eating dinner a little later.

It can also mean reserving time on weekends when it is more convenient to get together as a group, such as for Breakfast.

- **Five Color of Food a Day**

  Make it fun by having kids make a list of their favorite fruits and veggies and categorize them by color. Then, during each meal throughout the day, choose which ones they wish to eat, being sure to utilize different colors. They may keep track of what colors they eat on a daily basis and obtain a new colored sticker for each colored veggie they consume.

  Growing vegetables and herbs at home are enjoyable and teach children about the origins of food. Plant, water, weed, and, most importantly, eat your home-grown vegetables with your children or grandchildren. They will almost certainly take a bite off of anything they have grown themselves.

- **Helping While You Cook**

  Children of all ages can assist in the kitchen. Your kindergartener may not be able to chop veggies, but he or she can tear lettuce for a salad and place bread in a basket. Sauces can be stirred, and ingredients can be measured out by a 9- or 10-year-old.

When your grade-schooler matures into a teen who can skillfully prepare a delicious dinner for the whole family, you will be glad that you encouraged culinary practices early. These are the skills that are beneficial at all stages of life.

- **Respectful about Food**

  Maintaining a good attitude toward food and refraining from making disparaging remarks about your child's or anybody else's appearance or eating habits will assist build your child's relationship with food. Negative comments may be internalized by children, who may then food shame others or develop unhealthy eating patterns or disordered eating.

  Eating healthy food as much as possible, having lots of vegetables and fruits, and responding to your body's hunger and fullness cues should be the focus of positive dialogues.

  You can teach your youngster not to "yuck someone's yum" and not to make judgments about what other people eat. Another rule is that your child must try something before claiming he dislikes it.

- **Ask the Belly**

  Although children have the ability to stop eating when they are full, anxious parents often override this natural regulating mechanism in order to ensure that their children are eating the proper foods in sufficient quantities.

  Teach older children to pay attention to their stomachs and to ask themselves quantity and quality questions, such as, "Is my tummy full?" Will eating those extra biscuits make me sick? Is this really what my body requires right now?"

  The main goal is to make children aware of the numerous signs that tempt them to eat even when they are not hungry. Do kids really need to eat just because they are at the movies or walking through a shopping mall's food court?

- **Avoid Weight Conversations**

  Weight-related discussions with young kids can lead to low self-esteem, an unhealthy body image, and disordered eating in adolescence, when children are most vulnerable to these health problems, according to researchers.

According to a 2013 study, adolescents who had weight-related interactions with their parents were more likely to diet, engage in poor weight-control practices, and binge eat than those who only had good eating conversations with their parents.

Discuss good outcomes or behaviors that the youngster is interested in, such as athletic skills.

- **The Snack Plan**

Snacks are an excellent way to get nutrition into kids that they might not get at mealtime. Snacks are also useful when schedules are tight and/, or a meal is a long time away. Kids frequently respond more positively to snacks when they have a say in what they eat, just as they do with meals. Giving kids two snack options or allowing them to plan their snacks for the week can be beneficial.

It is also critical to consider the timing of snacks, which varies from family to family and child to child. In an ideal world, kids would consume snacks with enough time before a meal to feel hungry, so you need to take care of it.

- **No Forbidden Food**

  If you do not allow even a lollipop in your house, your child is more likely to eat "forbidden" food when they get the chance (at school or at a friend's house). It also conveys the impression that these restricted items are unique in some way.

  Avoid using terms like "good" or "bad," "healthy" or "unhealthy," "clean" or "junky," and so on while discussing foods. This is excellent practice for both children and adults.

  Including higher-sugar foods in a meal is a better approach to handle them. You could serve salad, spaghetti, and dessert to your youngster at the same time for dinner. This conveys the notion that each of these items is significant and that sweet foods are plentiful and not just restricted to lollipops and the likes.

  Allow children to consume the things on their plate in any sequence they like. Kids who have been denied sweets may have stronger reactions to this approach until they trust that the sweets will be available on a constant basis.

- **No Bribes**

  It is tempting to tell your child that they cannot have TV, dessert, or anything else unless they eat dinner, but this practice can lead to difficulties with a child's relationship with food. We want to teach kids to pay attention to their bodies. Bribing children to eat sends the message that it does not matter how they feel; what matters is what you say, not what their bodies are telling them.

  If your child refuses to eat because they dislike what is being offered, explain that this is dinner and that a snack will be available in about an hour. It is a good idea to provide at least one food your child likes with each meal, so they have something familiar to eat. They may be more willing to try new foods as a result of this.

4.2 Personal Hygiene and Care

The primary step in ensuring your child's health is to teach them the basics of personal hygiene. Healthy hygiene strengthens the immune system and minimizes the risk of contracting infections. Here are some strategies to help your child develop proper hygiene habits in order to prevent them from getting sick frequently:

- **Hand Hygiene**

Hand washing is the most essential and simple hygienic habit to develop. However, children often forget to wash their hands. It is your responsibility to remind the kids to wash their hands on a regular basis.

> ➢ Demonstrate how to thoroughly wash your hands.
> ➢ You should always urge your children to freshen up before handling any food or anything else when they arrive home from playing or school.
> ➢ Ask your children to wash their hands after petting an animal.
> ➢ It is essential to trim your nails because germs and dirt can accumulate under them. Furthermore, children have a proclivity for biting their nails, which you should discourage. Cut your child's nails on a regular basis and teach them how to do so since they should be able to do so around the age of seven.

You should also teach your children to wash their hands after each time they:

> ➢ Use the restroom.
> ➢ They should clean their room.
> ➢ Pay a visit to a sick family or acquaintance.

> They sneeze, cough, and blow their nose.

Hand washing is the most efficient and easiest way to keep germs and diseases at bay, and it takes less than a minute.

- **Oral Hygiene**

Oral hygiene is another vital aspect of personal hygiene that, if neglected, can lead to foul breath, cavities, and other oral disorders. All of this, however, can be avoided if your children practice basic oral hygiene. Here's how to go about it.

> Brush your child's teeth twice a day.

> Show them how to floss.

> Children love candies. However, it is vital to wash the mouth afterward. Remind your kids to do so after every mealtime.

> Tell your children to use mouthwash or gargle with warm salt water every now and again.

It is also a good idea to go to the dentist every six months.

- **Hair Hygiene**

Haircare is fundamental. Dandruff, head lice, and scalp infections can be caused by unkempt hair and poor grooming.

➢ Head lice are a common issue among children. As a result, you should instill in your children the habit of washing their hair at least twice a week.

➢ You should also teach your child not to share personal items with others, such as pillows, combs, and hats.

- **Bathing Hygiene**

The skin is our body's largest organ, and it protects us from a variety of germs and elements. If the skin is scratched or injured, it is also accessible to bacteria and other germs. Body smell and skin disorders such as infections with sensitive lumps and blisters can be caused by an excessive concentration of bacteria on the skin. To ensure your child's skin hygiene, you can perform the following:

➢ Teach your children to bathe every day. Showering before or after school, and certainly after playing outside, is essential.

➢ Teach them how to clean their armpits, hands, legs, joints, feet, back, elbows, belly button, and knees, among other body parts. You should demonstrate how to do it first and then allow them to practice.

➤ Make sure your children do not speed through their baths or showers because they may not clean themselves properly.

You must instill in your children the importance of personal cleanliness. You should begin teaching your children about germs and bacteria. Your children will have a better grasp of personal hygiene if they understand how they can get germs and what would happen if they do not maintain cleanliness. But do not make it too complicated or exaggerated, otherwise, they will develop a germ phobia.

Too much knowledge and directions regarding personal cleanliness will have no effect on your children. Because children's minds are unable to absorb all of the information, they may find the situation overwhelming.

As a result, you should begin with simple activities such as hand washing and bathing on a regular basis. Once the kids have gotten into the habit of practicing these tasks on a regular basis, you can move forward to the next fundamental hygiene job.

4.3 Healthy Consistent Sleeping

We all know how crucial proper sleep habits are for children. However, parents' hectic work schedules, after-school events, and schoolwork can all cut into family time on school evenings, affecting how much sleep a child gets. Given that many families' time together begins around 6 or 7 p.m. or even later on a school night, it might be difficult to establish an early bedtime. And, since school-age children require around 9-11 hours of sleep per night — which means they must go to bed around 9 p.m., depending on what time they must wake up — there is not much time left for anything other than schoolwork, dinner, and doing some reading together.

However, the amount of sleep a child gets has a significant impact on her growth and development. Less sleep has been proven to negatively affect a child's behavior, temperament, alertness, and ability to learn in studies. Sleep deprivation has been connected to poor performance on memory and attention tests in children. Sleep issues in elementary school were connected to poor performance on mental exams in adolescence, according to a study published in April 2009.

Use these points to help your child develop appropriate sleep habits and get a good night's sleep every night:

- **Model Behavior**

  Recognize the significance of getting enough sleep and how it affects your and your children's general health. Keep in mind that you are a role model for your child; lead by example.

  Pulling an all-nighter for work or staying up all night with your child to edit his or her paper is not the best way to communicate with your child. Making sleep a priority for yourself demonstrates to your children that it is an important aspect of having a healthy lifestyle, just like eating well and exercising on a regular basis.

- **Remove Electronic Stimulants**

  Allow at least an hour before night for your youngster to use the computer, watch TV or check her phone. These screen activities can be stimulating and can make it difficult to fall and stay asleep.

- **Sleep Supportive Environment**

  Adjust the temperature of the house and dim the bright lights before going to bed. Filling your child's bed with toys is not a good idea. Keep your child's bed as a sleeping area rather than a play area. A comfort blanket or a favorite doll or teddy is acceptable and can help with separation anxiety.

- **Set a Routine**

   When it comes to teaching excellent sleep habits in children, a good nighttime routine is vital. Whatever your evening ritual is—a bath, brushing teeth, pajamas, and reading a few pages from a book—make sure to keep to it every night so that your child knows what to anticipate and can smoothly proceed through each routine.

- **Avoid Caffeine**

   You would not deny a cup of coffee to a grade-schooler before bedtime, but it can be found in unexpected food items, such as bottled tea, chocolate, and even some non-cola sodas. When it is near bedtime, avoid foods that contain caffeine, and if your child requests dessert, stick to nutritious fruit.

- **Consistency**

   We cannot make up for lost sleep. A health expert explains that Sleep is not like a bank in the sense that you cannot build up a debt and hope to pay it off later. As adults, many of us do the same thing, sleeping less during the week and making up for it on weekends. The issue is that this is not consistent sleep.

According to health experts, having 5 hours of sleep during the week and 8-10 hours on the weekends is linked to an unhealthy lifestyle and raises our risk of high blood pressure and diabetes. It is critical for parents to develop a consistent sleep regimen for their children.

- **Sleep Challenge**

  You can set up a sleep challenge as a class or as a family by having each participant keep track of how many hours of sleep, they got each night and when they went to bed. The person with the highest sleep-time average and bedtime consistency after a week is named "Learner of the week."

- **Sleep Journal**

  Encourage your child to make connections between how well they sleep, what they do before going to sleep, and how they feel when they wake up by using their sleep journal template. This template can be printed in numerous copies to assist your child keep track of their sleep and compare days when they slept well to days when they did not.

4.4 Physical Activities and Exercise

Do you know that just about one out of every four children get the necessary 60 minutes of daily physical activity? As a child's age and his grade in school changes, so does their participation in all sorts of physical activity. Physical activity should be a component of family life on a daily basis.

Being physically active entails moving sufficiently to cause heavy breathing, shortness of breath, and sweating. Children's health and well-being are dependent on physical activity. Physical activity, for example, aids in the development and maintenance of healthy muscles, bones, and joints. It can help you maintain a healthy BMI and lower your risk of diabetes, hypertension, and heart disease later in life. It can assist kids in falling asleep quickly and sleeping soundly.

Physical activity promotes a child's emotional and behavioral health in addition to physical benefits. It improves a child's school achievement, self-esteem, focus, and conduct by increasing their excitement and optimism. Anxiety, stress, and sadness are also reduced. Organized sport can help promote teamwork and friendship. Here are some ways you can develop a habit of being active and fit in your kids:

- **Move Together**

  Every night after dinner, your family should ideally get up and engage in some type of physical activity as a family. It could be anything as small as going for a stroll, riding bikes, or playing catch. It does not matter what activity you engage in as long as you are all moving together. If nighttime does not fit into your schedule, consider if you can be active together at a different time of day. Starting with 15 minutes per day is a good place to start.

- **Prioritize Walking**

  Instead of sitting in a car, get the kids moving as much as possible. If a safe path exists, have them walk or bike to school every day (if they are too young to walk or ride on their own). This is an excellent habit to develop at a young age. Remember to leave enough time to reach where you need to be so you do not have to rush.

- **Focus on Fun**

  Recognize when your child is having fun with some activity and encourage them. Maintain a positive attitude from the sidelines, so they know that you appreciate what they are doing but are not too immersed in it to put them under strain.

Most children are not ready to compete until they are ten years old. Non-competitive games and fun activities keep things stress-free for kids under ten and allow them to succeed regardless of their ability level.

- **Active Screen Time**

  When going outside to play is not a choice, your kids can play interactive video games like bowling, tennis, or baseball that require physical exertion. You can also use active video games and dance videos to get some physical activity while they are on screens.

- **Any Activity with Movement**

  Organized sports, such as baseball, hockey, or soccer, are not for everyone. Other hobbies that your youngster might love include rock climbing, swimming, and martial arts. And be patient; finding the proper fit for your child may take some trial and error.

  When your child is not having fun anymore, it is probably time to consider another option. Keep experimenting with different concepts until you find something that works. Non-athletic children must be motivated and active in order to develop a lifelong habit of physical activity.

- **Participate with Your Kids**

  When parents play with their kids, mostly they are ecstatic. Plan more outside activities with the family to brighten their spirits and make them feel relaxed and at ease. If you have a pet, take him on a hike with your child or engage in a gardening activity with him, which will re-energize your child. Take a family hike to encourage your child's fitness. Play a game of catch with your friends. Play hopscotch as you walk or bike to school. You do not need a lot of expensive equipment or special lessons to get your child to exercise.

4.5 Healthy Hydration

Even slight dehydration can affect a child's health and performance negatively. Dehydration can cause you to lose as little as 2% of your body weight, which can damage your alertness, memory, response time, and thinking. This is important for students who need to be able to concentrate and study in order to succeed in school.

How can you tell if your child is dehydrated? Headaches, weariness, irritability, and dizziness are all common symptoms.

Urine color (dark yellow urine is a common symptom) and urinating less than every 2-4 hours are two key markers. To put it in another way, if your child goes an entire school day without peeing, he or she is most likely dehydrated. Let's see how we can resolve this:

- **Show Them**

  Modeling appropriate hydration habits for your child is one of the most effective methods to teach them. Avoiding sugary drinks or juices in favor of plain water demonstrates to your children what optimal hydration looks like in practice.

- **Make it Fun**

  Drinking water can be made more appealing to your child by using amusing, colorful straws or sippy cups. There are various handy gadgets on the market for children that can make drinking water feel like an exciting adventure for them.

  It can also be beneficial to set up a station with a drip-free pitcher, straws, water bottles, and cups where your children can hydrate themselves anytime they want. Giving kids control over their hydration makes for a more thorough learning experience and encourages them to listen to their bodies.

If your toddler prefers the taste of juice over water, make amusing ice cubes out of frozen fruits to vary the flavor slightly. For Lego fans, Star Wars fans, and creative children (You can use stars, suns, trees, sea life, and flowers), there are trays that make amazing cubes. For a bit of taste and a splash of color, use plain rectangular ice and add mint leaves, fruit, or a splash of fruit juice. Instead of putting fruit on ice, you may do what beach resorts and premium spas do and put it straight in your water. Infuse your water with sliced fruits or berries directly in your pitcher, or use a water bottle with a built-in infuser.

- **Use Fruit and Vegetables**

Many vegetables and fruits can help you stay hydrated because they have high water content. Cantaloupe, watermelon, strawberries, grapefruit, and blueberries are among the most popular fruits. Zucchini, cucumber, iceberg lettuce, tomato, and celery are some of the greatest vegetables to choose from.

- **Sugary Drinks and Juices**

The American Academy of Pediatrics suggests not giving sugary drinks to children under the age of two. Sodas, Whole fruit juices, and sports hydration drinks all fall within this category.

Between the ages of one and three, just four ounces of juice should be consumed every day. Older children can drink more juice, but if whole fruits are unavailable, juice should be used instead.

- **Easy Access**

Make water easily accessible for your child to encourage them to drink more water. Purchase water bottles in children's sizes to make it easier for your youngster to hold them and have them on hand throughout the day.

- **Use Applications**

You can get a water reminder and tracking app for your child if they have a smartphone or tablet. The idea is to make remembering the water intake enjoyable rather than frightening or punishing.

There are many free and paid options available, but here are a few of the more kid-friendly options:

> ➤ **Plant Nanny**

Choose a seedling and support its growth by keeping track of your water consumption. Because this is a free app, it contains advertisements and upsells. It also lacks the features of other hydration apps, such as reminders. Still, it is entertaining, and it adds a visual element to the process of drinking water.

> ➤ **Carbodroid.**

Instead of a plant, use this Android app to power up a charming tiny robot. It also has a basic, user-friendly layout and provides reminders.

Check to see if your child is not using any water tracking applications that include diet culture messaging or link water consumption to weight, body size, or other factors.

4.6 Table Manner Habits

Good table manners for kids are a crucial aspect of any meal, whether you are eating at home, enjoying dinner with friends, or dining out. When you educate your child on proper mealtime manners, you are providing them with valuable social skills that will be beneficial for them for the rest of their lives. Moreover, a lack of good etiquette can lead to the spread of germs and infections. We may also control portion sizes for ourselves and our children by eating from a plate at a table. When we do not use technology during meals, we eat more mindfully. We are more likely to enjoy our meal if we pay attention to it. Watching television while eating causes you to eat more but enjoy your food less.

Every meal provides an opportunity for children to practice basic etiquette. Little children can learn how to be respectful and exhibit table manners by using their utensils properly and waiting until everyone has been served.

Here are some simple lessons you can start teaching your children:

- **Clean Hands**

  Teach your kids to wash up before dinner. This not only shows respect for the person who made the meal as well as the other guests at the table. It is also a good hygiene practice.

- **Chewing with Mouth Closed**

  Two basic rules of good table manners are chewing with your mouth closed and not chatting when your mouth is full. If your child forgets, gently remind him.

- **Wait for Others**

  Teach your child to be patient until everyone is seated and served at the table before starting to eat. It is impolite to eat before everyone has been seated. Dinner is supposed to be shared with others.

- **No Electronics**

  Mealtime is about more than just eating. It is all about making connections with the people you are dining with and sharing an experience with them. That is difficult to accomplish when your child's face is hidden behind a screen.

  Teach children that bringing devices to the table is not only impolite, but it also means that they are missing out on togetherness and connection.

- **Avoid Reaching**

  Remind your child that reaching over the table to acquire something is never a good idea. Make it a practice to ask others at the table to pass something they require.

- **No Stuffing**

  Ask your child to take small bites so they can chew properly and avoid digestive problems.

- **As to Be Excused**

  Most preferably, children should stick to the dinner table until everyone is done. However, it is also okay to ask for permission to leave if they have finished, but the grownups are still lingering and talking.

These are six habits your child can adopt for a healthy body, ultimately supporting a healthy mind.

Chapter 5: Keeping the Nasty Away

Children might develop some unhealthy habits and behaviors. It is easier to change an unpleasant habit if you first figure out why your child is doing it. Bad behaviors are usually just a coping mechanism. When your child is bored, stressed, sad, frustrated, weary, or insecure, they may resort to these behaviors. For children, many of the "bad" habits are relaxing and pleasant. Some unhealthy habits might have a negative impact on a child's growth and development. As a result, it is critical to urge children to break undesirable habits as soon as feasible. However, bad habits need to be replaced with good habits for the process to really work, and it is hard to make good habits stick. Let's get into the details.

5.1 Bad Habits They Won't Go Away

We want our kids to have healthy and long lives. Unfortunately, today's kids appear to be less active, have a bad diet, and spend more time playing video games and toying with other technologies. However, these are lifestyle patterns that parents and children can change with some effort. In truth, a few small modifications can make a significant difference in your children's health. Which habits do you need to be vigilant of in your kids? Read below:

Common Bad Habits in Kids

Here are a few of the undesirable habits that many children have:

- **Poor Sleep**

  Getting enough sleep is a crucial part of maintaining a healthy lifestyle. According to new research, sleep disorders in children, such as sleep apnea, are linked to behavioral issues, poor academic performance, and obesity. According to a Spanish study, children who do not receive enough sleep are more likely to have memory and language issues. Another study found that poor nighttime habits were linked to low self-esteem, tantrums, and, in certain cases, ADHD misdiagnosis.

- **Bad Hygiene**

  Children are not always as sanitary as we would like, and puberty can make things even worse. If your kid participates in sports or is physically active, hygiene is even more crucial. Personal cleanliness habits are linked to fewer illnesses and improved health. Poor personal hygiene, on the other hand, can result in minor adverse effects such as body odor and oily skin. They can potentially lead to more problematic or even life-threatening problems.

If you do not wash your hands frequently, for example, germs and bacteria can readily enter your mouth or eyes. This can cause many problems, ranging from pink eye to stomach viruses.

Tooth decay and plaque buildup can result from not brushing your teeth. Poor dental hygiene is connected to a number of major health problems, including heart disease.

Self-esteem can be harmed by poor hygiene habits. Looking and feeling tidy can enhance your confidence and make you feel good about yourself.

Practice good personal hygiene to avoid or reduce the risk of other conditions. The following are some examples:

- Pubic Lice
- Scabies
- Head Lice
- Diarrhea
- Body Lice
- Athlete's Foot
- Pinworms
- Ringworm
- Swimmer's Ear

- **Procrastination**

Procrastination is an unhealthy behavior that can easily be carried over into adulthood. Teenagers may not have as many duties to delay as adults, but homework and chores are frequently the things that are postponed. The issue is that the promised "later" time never arrives.

Students' academics, grades, and even their general well-being can suffer as a result of procrastination. Procrastinating students suffer higher levels of irritation, guilt, tension, and worry, which can lead to major concerns such as depression and low self-esteem. Procrastination's impacts on high school kids can be even more severe. Students who wait until the last minute, obtain lower grades than their classmates after they enter high school and begin receiving more take-home tasks and larger projects.

This can provoke a vicious cycle of poor grades and low self-esteem, which is difficult for pupils to break. This can lead to immense frustration and stress as kids' grades begin to affect their post-secondary possibilities.

- **Poor Eating**

  According to a new report from Michigan, one out of every four third-graders in the state is overweight, and one out of every eleven is obese.

  It is easy to see why if you look around the grocery store at items marketed to school children. Nutritional deficiency has become a big issue. A recent study examined 367 items marketed to children and found that 89 percent of them were of poor nutritional content due to high quantities of sugar, fat, or salt.

  In a young child, the rate of nutrient absorption and utilization is extremely high. His growth may be hampered if she does not take proper care when preparing her nutrition. His muscle strength and visual acuity, as well as the growth of her bones and teeth, improve significantly. Obesity is caused by a high intake of nutritionally deficient foods, which leads to long-term disorders such as hypertension, diabetes, and cancer. The most prevalent side effects of diets lacking in magnesium and calcium, as well as increased consumption of simple carbohydrates, include early childhood tooth decay (ECTD), regular muscle cramps, and deformed bones (e.g., knock knees and bow knees.)

- **Poor Exercise**

  According to a World Health Organization survey, 80 percent of children aged 11 to 17 are insufficiently physically active. Lack of physical activity in early life can result in a variety of health issues. Weight gain, excess body fat, high blood pressure, cardiovascular disorders, poor cholesterol, and bone health issues are just a few of these issues. Physical activities have more health benefits than drawbacks. Children who participate in physical activities have a lower risk of developing chronic health conditions. They are less likely to become ill. They have a lower risk of developing a variety of ailments, including diabetes, heart disease, depression, obesity, and mental illness.

- **Electronic Overload**

  According to AAP, the American Academy of Pediatrics, the average youngster spends seven hours each day staring at a screen, whether it is a computer, mobile phone, television, or other electronic devices.

  We may not realize it, but children's brains are significantly more vulnerable to electronics than we think. Excessive screen usage has been related to school troubles, hostility, and other behavioral issues.

Sensory overload causes children to lose focus and depletes their mental energy, leading to rage and erratic conduct. Kids can become overstimulated and "revved up," making it difficult for them to manage stress and regulate their mood.

Too much screen time can also impair your child's sleep, resulting in mood swings and cognitive problems. A youngster who spends too much time in front of a computer has less time for active, imaginative play and exercise, which puts them at risk for obesity and mental problems.

The impacts of excessive screen time on children's psychological well-being were examined in one study, according to the AAP. The findings showed that youngsters who spent more than two hours per day in front of a screen, regardless of physical activity, had more psychological troubles.

These are some of the negative habits that can temper your child's physical and mental health. Have you noticed that bad habits are so tempting compared to good ones? Have you ever thought why? Have you thought why breaking habits is so hard?

Dopamine plays a huge factor in this.

Pleasure and Bad Habits

Dopamine is a brain neurotransmitter that makes us feel good. Dopamine, along with other chemicals like oxytocin, serotonin, and endorphins, interacts with the pleasure and reward center of our brain and influences how joyful we feel. Dopamine influences our mobility, memory, and focus in addition to our mood. Low levels of dopamine can negatively affect us physically and psychologically, while high levels encourage us to seek out and repeat pleasurable activities.

We feel good when the brain has a healthy level of dopamine. Our desire to succeed grows. We get things done. We are quick learners. We are motivated, enthusiastic about life, aware, and focused. Dopamine levels that are normal can make us more gregarious and extroverted. This "feel good" neurotransmitter also aids in the development of empathy for others, making us more adaptable to their demands. Dopamine can also help you be more creative. All of these characteristics contribute to the pleasurable feelings associated with dopamine. However, when the brain does not have enough dopamine, our motivation plunges, our emotions shift, and our conduct can deteriorate dramatically.

Dopamine interacts with brain cells, encouraging them to behave in excitable, pleasurable, and euphoric ways. One of the reasons that dopamine motivates us is its excitatory properties. Dopamine regulates our behavior by urging our brain cells to perform certain behaviors.

Our bodies release dopamine in response to pleasurable experiences such as eating satisfying food, sexual engagement, or drug usage. Our brain subsequently correlates dopamine release with pleasure, resulting in the creation of a reward system. When you consume comfort food, for example, your brain produces dopamine, which makes you feel happy.

So, your brain interprets this as a reward and encourages you to continue doing so, despite the fact that soothing food may not be the healthiest option for your body.

Dopamine is linked to positive reinforcement. It is supposed to be the chemical that makes a person want to do something over and over again. We develop our personal habits with the help of reward and reinforcement. Positive experiences are preferred by humans, whereas negative experiences are avoided. Dopamine is the chemical behind these patterns. Okay, so we have learned that dopamine is released whenever we enjoy something. Our brain helps us to receive that pleasure again and again by making it a habit through dopamine.

How can we help our children break their dopamine-proved bad habits and sometimes just subconscious bad habits?

Let's understand this step by step in a bit more detail.

Breaking Bad Habits

Let me explain:

- **Begin with Understanding**

First, try to comprehend your child's actions. What is their source?

Children are innocent and oblivious, and bad habits are usually a kind of self-soothing. Adults find nose picking to be one of the most revolting habits. A child does not pick their nose to offend you; they do it to get to the crust that irritates them.

When a youngster has allergies or a dry nasal cavity, he or she is more likely to pick their nose. Understand the problem and fix it. Treat your child's allergies, clean up the dusty environment, keep him hydrated, and make it a private joke.

Educate your child on how rude and nasty it is, how boogers transmit hundreds of germs that can make you sick, and that if you have to do it, do it in the bathroom. The child will learn that picking one's nose is not socially acceptable and causes shame with time and gentle reminders.

Biting and striking are two more habits that parents are concerned about. Toddlers and preschoolers frequently have difficulty expressing themselves and their feelings, and they lash out in frustration as a result. If you do not give children enough attention, they might resort to violent behavior.

To avoid violence, gently but firmly explain to your child that striking is not acceptable behavior and that you will not tolerate it. Instead of yelling, give them a time-out and remind them that they need to apologize.

Observe and learn what usually triggers such behavior in your child.

Is it a result of too much exposure to the screen or television? Is it a clingy playmate or a problem with sharing toys? Is it hunger or a lack of sleep? After you have recognized the root reasons, you will be able to deal with them more effectively.

- **Come Up with Solution**

  Come up with alternatives to your child's habit once you have identified what is causing it. Allow him to squeeze a stress ball instead of biting his nails if homework makes him nervous.

Lay down with him and lovingly hold his hand if he wants the comfort of thumb sucking when he is drowsy. What about a child that has a propensity of acting out his or her excitement in a non-acceptable manner? Before he gets worked up, calmly remind him that biting is not an option.

- **Work as a Team**

  When you are educating or pressing your child to break harmful behaviors, you instantly go to the opposite direction and become "against" him, which is the last thing you want. Work with your child to help them develop stronger, more powerful, and more self-controllable, as well as to help them break harmful habits.

- **Gently Point and Remind**

  This method can be used with children as young as three or four years old to help raise awareness of the situation. Something along the lines of, "When you do not sleep at time, your whole routine gets disturbed. You cannot play or study like you should because of not getting enough sleep. Do you understand?"

Try not to nag your youngster after you have talked to them about breaking the habit. Punishment, criticism, or ridicule may lead to an increase in undesirable conduct. Instead, if you spot them engaging in their habit, send them a modest signal to inform them of the habit's replacement alternative.

- **Encourage Them**

  When you compliment a child on their good manners, they smile at you with such a charming smile. Use it as a motivator to get them to practice good behaviors. Appreciate if you are using a reward chart, congratulate them on their good behavior and offer them a modest reward. When they fall into poor behaviors, consciously ignore them to express your dissatisfaction.

  Encouragement and praise enhance their spirits and motivate them to do well. Your disapproval, on the other hand, will make them feel ashamed and guilty. It is a great method for breaking a variety of bad habits.

- **Take it Slow**

  Frequently, children establish a number of negative behaviors at the same time. Do not try to tackle them all at once. Take it one step at a time.

Begin with the most harmful one, such as bullying or lying, and do everything you can to eliminate it. From the standpoint of consideration, reason and explain cause and effect, actions' consequences, and negative behavior. You may think your child is little, but they actually know and understand a lot more than we think.

- **Be Discreet**

    Discuss, reason, and explain. Do not embarrass your children by discussing their troubles in front of others. It will only cause them to lose faith in you. Children must see their parents as someone they can rely on in order to assist them. They will continue to trust you and find it easier to confide in you and listen to you if you protect their privacy and provide a safe, supportive, and caring environment.

The next section is about if you become successful in replacing a bad habit with a good one how you can avoid relapse.

5.2 Good Habits: They Won't Stick

It is so simple to fall into bad habits. They are not only simple, but they are also occasionally more enjoyable — though only for a short time. Your negative habits are a part of your life, even if you have a love-hate relationship with them. They are like that old buddy you need to bid farewell to but do not want to hurt their feelings. Secondly, we expect too much and forget that change takes time and patience. It takes 66 days on average to form a habit. Here is what you can do to help your kids make their good habits stick:

- **It Needs to Be Simple**

  Focusing on one habit at a time is more likely to be successful than attempting to deal with everything at once, whether you wish to make or break your child's behaviors. For example, instead of focusing on "everything" that needs to change, you are more likely to succeed if you focus on one or two incorrect habits you would like to modify.

  Once you have decided what needs to change, breaking it down into small, regular steps makes it easier to manage and increases your chances of success. Consider it for a moment.

If you want to create an article, split it down into manageable chunks — introduction, a major body, conclusion - and focus on each section individually rather than the full essay.

You do not lose weight just by declaring, "I want to lose weight." You lose weight by taking little, daily steps: on Tuesday, Wednesday, and Thursday, I will run for 20 minutes. Alternatively, only eat cheese on weekends.

The same rule is true when it comes to assisting children in forming or breaking habits. Expecting too much too soon is more likely to fail than asking your child to read a book or paint for 10 minutes every day.

- **Stick to the Rules**

  The precise sequence of steps we choose in our routine, as well as the rules we choose to form that routine, are not nearly as crucial as sticking to it. When it comes to developing a habit, consistency is key. So, at least for the first few times, focus on being consistent, even if it is inconvenient.

If during the morning routine you need your child to develop a healthy breakfast habit after getting dressed up, it means that you will have to make sure breakfast is ready by the time your kids get dressed, even if it means getting up a bit earlier to do so. The purpose is that you find the right combination of convenience and practicality for your families and then follow the guidelines.

- **Positive Reinforcement**

Positive reinforcement helps, but only when it is done correctly. Remember to rejoice in even the tiniest achievements because it is these that will encourage your child.

The use of "tricks" like a reward chart to encourage good conduct has also been demonstrated to be highly beneficial, particularly with young children. Incentive charts are particularly useful because they encourage youngsters to be active participants (for example, your child can be in charge of pasting a sticker on the chart every time he earns a point) and make achieving the desired behavior more enjoyable.

An incentive chart works by picking one specific behavior and awarding a certain number of points each time your child exhibits it.

You then total up the points on a weekly or daily basis to calculate the prize your child will receive when a certain number of points is reached.

Our brain uses the reward to decide whether or not a routine is worth remembering.

Most individuals believe that the reward is the most important component and concentrate solely on it. However, in my experience, the reward is the least important component of the puzzle.

Do not get me wrong: it is a necessary component to get things started. However, once a habit is formed, we may easily remove the incentive, and the habit will survive. So you do not need to be concerned about setting a perfect reward.

So, for the time being, choose any incentive that you believe will be beneficial to your family. Anything you can deliver on is fine, whether it is a trip to the zoo, a sticker chart, or a visit to the park. However, keep in mind that everything we do as a parent is based on trust. It goes without saying that if parents promise a reward, they must deliver - rain or sunshine.

- **Build Routine with Margin**

  Parents know that things do not always go as planned as parents. For example, in your morning routine, there will be one sock that has mysteriously vanished, spilled milk to clean, the water bottle will begin to leak, and the lunch bag handle will break, and pretty much anything that may go wrong will do so at some point. We will need to leave some room to digest these.

- **Develop Craving**

  Craving is the most critical step of the habit loop. The desire is what drives us to repeat the routine over and over until it becomes deeply embedded in our brain's memory circuit, to the point that we will continue to do so even if the reward is taken away at a later time. When it comes to cravings, there are two factors at play: the "artificial" cravings that are induced by the reward we choose and the "natural" cravings that are induced naturally.

  The tangible joy from receiving the reward is the "artificial" craving. The "natural" desire, on the other hand, is intangible yet incredibly rewarding. Even here, there are two levels: the first is the child's desire for parental love and approval.

The underlying, fundamental satisfaction that every person feels when they do the right thing for the right reasons is the next level.

Our goal is to begin with, artificial craving and gradually guide them toward becoming more intrinsically motivated.

- **Acknowledge with Praise**

Wait for the moment when you notice your child doing something well and take advantage of the opportunity to show your joy. You do not have to be giddy or overly enthusiastic. Just make sure you acknowledge it positively with a smile, pat on the back, hug, or other gesture. Returning to our morning routine scenario above, if you make it out the door without any issues, you can add something like, "You were so speedy with your breakfast today! Thanks to your efforts, we will get out on time, and we will be able to rest a lot more on the way to school.

- **Set Realistic Expectations**

Children should be motivated to learn from their mistakes. Planning realistic goals and keeping restrictions in mind are essential for any new behavior to stick.

Small changes over time can make a major difference in your behaviors, so start small and work your way up. As parents, you must understand that each child develops at his or her unique pace.

Children dislike being told what they cannot do, so tell them what they can. Keep it lighthearted and upbeat. Everyone enjoys being complimented on a job well done. Celebrate accomplishments while also assisting children and teens in developing a good self-image.

- **Do not Give up**

Lack of consistency is one of the major reasons we cannot seem to break bad habits or create new ones. We all know that it is hard to stay consistent all of the time and that things do not always go according to plan. The quickest route to failure is to give up.

Reflect on what motivated you to try to change your child's habits when you are weary and irritated. What research and resources did you use to make the decision to attempt something new? Return to them and read them again. Consider how changing that behavior – or developing a new one – will benefit you. Reminiscing about how you got started can help you get back on track.

Hopefully, these strategies will help you develop good and healthy habits in your kids and assure that bad habits do not bounce back.

Conclusion

Humans are the creatures who like to stick to their routines. Our brains enjoy automating a series of procedures to develop a habit since it frees up space for all of the other crucial decision-making processes. Healthy behaviors, such as getting up at five a.m. to go for a run before work, can coexist with less-than-ideal habits, such as munching on a packet of chips while watching TV or reaching for a drink to unwind.

Indulging once in a while will not have a significant impact. However, our brains are hardwired to desire to repeat routines, especially if there is a reward at the end, such as a dopamine or endorphin rush. These habits, when repeated again and over, have a beneficial or negative impact on our health and well-being. Our health is dependent on our habits. They control our chances of accomplishing and sustaining our lifestyle goals, such as sticking to a diet, managing diabetes and other health issues, frequently exercising, as well as improving quality of life, and enhancing lifespan. Obesity and diabetes are linked to bad behaviors such as increased intake of sugary soft drinks and fast food, as well as low levels of physical exercise.

However, maintaining healthy habits, such as eating enough fruits, vegetables, and fresh foods and exercising regularly, can be extremely advantageous to one's health. Healthy behaviors can aid in blood sugar control and the prevention of diseases such as diabetes and cancer.

Habits are unconsciously performed acts and behaviors that are extremely difficult to break. This is because the chemical dopamine is released into the brain when we create and repeat routines, resulting in a pleasurable experience and a stronger habit. This is why it is critical for your children to start developing healthy behaviors at a young age. Realizing this need during my own parenthood, I decided to write this book focused on some fundamental physical and mental habits for children. The first chapter deals with the four parenting styles, i.e., authoritarian, authoritative, permissive, and uninvolved, and their characteristics and effects on children. This step will help you determine your parenting styles and make adjustments accordingly while you support your children in making or breaking habits. Furthermore, the chapter will include common parenting mistakes which you have to avoid in the habit-building or breaking process.

You will find under this heading mistakes such as not exhibiting model behavior, making up lies, not acknowledging good behavior, realizing what is not working, fighting back, making idle threats, setting unrealistic expectations, and tricking your children.

The next chapter is devoted to building an understanding of healthy habits. The chapter will entail the meaning and importance of healthy habits, why do we need habits, how habits are built and how you can break your child's bad habits. Moving on, the importance of developing the right habits at a young age has been discussed.

The third and fourth chapter includes more than ten healthy habits for nourishing the mind and the body of children. The habits for a healthy mind include active communication, time management, discipline and self-control, emotional intelligence, problem solving and creative thinking, effective learning, and being constructive in teamwork. The habits for a healthy body include healthy, nutritious eating, personal hygiene and care, healthy, consistent sleeping, physical activities and exercise, healthy hydration, and table manners habits. All of these habits will be discussed in detail as to how you can incorporate them into your child's life.

The last and fifth chapter focuses on the phycology of bad habits and what are some common bad habits of youngsters and how to avoid them. In the last chapter of the book, there will be some more insight into breaking bad habits for your children. In the end, the chapter will discuss how you can make the good habits stick, so the bad habits do not bounce back. A simple routine, sticking to the rules, allowing margin in routine, positive reinforcement, develop a craving, acknowledging with praise and being realistic towards goals, and not giving up will be discussed in this section.

Parenting my first child inspired me to write this book, and I have written it with my professional and personal knowledge on parenting. This book is a gift to all the parents new to parenthood and will help them raise healthy and smart children.

If this book has met your expectations, please leave a review on Amazon.

www.ingramcontent.com/pod-product-compliance
Lightning Source LLC
Chambersburg PA
CBHW022101020426
42335CB00012B/787